Praise for

"Honesty and clarity are the pr
offers these qualities so natura
personal presence ... unhurriec

~Fred Chappell, Bollingen Prize for Poetry

"...poems full of family feeling. Honeycutt is a survivor who takes her grief and ruminations ... into isolated settings.... We go with her into a landscape she makes familiar."

~Maxine Kumin, Pulitzer Prize for Poetry

"...poems like Wordsworth's 'spots of time' ... finely attuned to Nature's beauties and terrors. A painterly poet, full of sharply realized observations."

~Peter Meinke, inaugural Poet Laureate of St. Petersburg, Florida

"Among the things poetry can do is to help us celebrate, help us mourn.... [Her] poems range from the prose-like to the formal, from details of life and death to small lyric moments."

~Linda Pastan, Ruth Lilly Poetry Prize

"Irene Honeycutt defies the easy stereotype of Poet, disengaged from everyday life. Even better, she defies it with a vengeance—an energy that enlivens her work throughout."

~Kathryn Stripling Byer, North Carolina Poet Laureate 2005-2009

"...the heart repairing itself through her authentic voice...."

~Julie Suk, author of *Lie Down with Me: New and Selected Poems*

"One of North Carolina's finest poets."

~Ron Rash, author of *Poems: New & Selected*

"I love this poem ['Blessing'] because it evokes so hauntingly the end of so many of my summers in different cities, different countries."

~George Bilgere, Cleveland Arts Prize

"For over half a century, Irene Honeycutt has crafted stunning, cinematic poems with the wise, loving insight of the contemplative—and an eye, ear, and heart pitched precisely to the very soul of poetry. The appearance of a new collection by her is a signature, celebratory moment; and it should surprise no one that her latest volume, *Mountains of the Moon*, is her absolute finest to date. A virtuoso with narrative, the lyric and hybrid forms, Honeycutt's range is incomparable and the risks she takes with language are often unimaginable, always transformative. The yield of *Mountains of the Moon* is so lustrous— "something / bright and unforeseen on the horizon"—that one is evangelized by its prismatic brilliance, the abundant, reckoning light."

~Joseph Bathanti, North Carolina Poet Laureate 2012-2014

Mountains
of the Moon

Also by Irene Blair Honeycutt

Beneath the Bamboo Sky
Before the Light Changes
Waiting for the Trout to Speak
It Comes as a Dark Surprise

Mountains of the Moon

Poems & Pieces

Irene Blair Honeycutt

Charlotte Center for Literary Arts, Inc.
Charlotte, North Carolina
charlottelit.org

Copyright © 2024 by Irene Blair Honeycutt
All rights reserved

ISBN: 978-1-960558-09-1

Library of Congress Control Number: 2024945584

Cover Image: Erica Fielder, *Mountains of the Moon,* 1983. Original watercolor
    painting, copyright © 1983 by Erica Fielder, used with permission.
    EricaFielderStudio.com.
Author photo by Peggy Brooks
Book design and layout by Paul Reali

Charlotte Lit Press
Charlotte Center for Literary Arts, Inc.
PO Box 18607, Charlotte, NC 28218
charlottelit.org/press

PROUD MEMBER

COMMUNITY OF LITERARY MAGAZINES & PRESSES
W W W . C L M P . O R G

For my teachers — the best of them

Indissolubly connected ... The once the now the then and again
~C. D. Wright

Contents

To the Reader   i

One

During the Time of No Moon   3

Reading Time   4

Indelible   5

Footsteps   6

Pandemic Guests   7

I Felt a Forest Growing in My Skin   8

Talking to Siri in Pandemic Time   9

Tea at My Potter Friend's *Wind Gather* Cabin,
   Jonas Ridge NC   10

Heron   12

It Can Happen Anywhere   13

Praying Mantis on the Patio   14

Cold Long Night, 2020   15

Song for the Hours   16

Two

Sky Turtle   21

When You See a Shelf Mushroom   22

Salt   23

In the Sunlight of Enchantment   24

Maybe It Was Nott   25

In the Dentist's Waiting Room, 2018   26

The Roofers   28

I Drive Old Monroe Road   29

Milkweed, Jonas Ridge NC   30

Three

Remembering Linda Pastan 33

Collage for a Friend in Grief 35

Song for the Sea Lion, Steep Ravine CA 36

Remembering Miroslav Holub *from Some Symphonic Distance* 38

Legacy, 2020 40

Four

Another Wandering Aengus 45

You Entered My Car Years Later 46

The Rug 47

Without Feathers 48

Talisman 49

Easter, and the pear trees blossom 51

Ashes 52

Beginning an Elegy 53

A Way into the Trees 56

Five

Words 59

Poetry Reading at an Indian Trail Cafe 60

Cicada, I Never Knew You Were the Loudest Insect
    in the World Until I Read 62

Leaves, Curbside 64

Email Morning 65

Octopus Farming for the Food Harvest 66

One Peppermint Ball 67

When the Challenge Came in Fifth Grade 69

Ten Years Old and She No Longer Believes in Santa 70

Joy 72

Six

Moon 77
When the Last Page Turns 78
Each Morning, the Fall 79
A Dream That Still Makes Me Cry 80
Why, among My Brothers 81
The Dead Don't Miss Us 82
The House within a Mansion 84
Landlines and Train Tracks 86
Adobe House, Taos 87
Mama was Clever 88
Ars Poetica 90
Beyond the Iron Gate 91
I Asked Rilke's Darkest Angels 93

Seven

We Came to a Place that was Grieving
   and Gathered to Listen 97
Total Solar Eclipse, 2024 103

Notes 105
Poem Dedications 107
Acknowledgments 109
About the Author 111

To the Reader

Time is but the stream I go a-fishing in. I drink at it; but while I drink I see the sandy bottom and detect how shallow it is. Its thin current slides away, but eternity remains. I would drink deeper; fish in the sky, whose bottom is pebbly with stars.

~Henry David Thoreau

The stream of time brings its treasures to our feet and places them before our eyes.

I've paused on many bridges when hiking through woods and stared into streams, watching for what would draw me in. Once, I thought I saw a fish swimming upside down until the cottonmouth swam to the edge and crawled up a rock, holding the catch in its mouth. Staring into the streams, I also listened. Mesmerized by calming ripples or excited by stormy froths rushing over rocks, I learned how to imagine the pulse of river rocks I held in my hands.

The poet Margaret Gibson sees the art of writing poetry as "an act of attention and receptivity. You study whatever it is that strikes your attention—whether a scarlet tanager, river, field, or forest; whether mother, daughter, alcoholic, photographer, lover. You take what's given into that part of the self that inquires, tests, embraces, and embodies. Outer and inner coalesce and fuse."

An example of what Gibson is saying occurs while I'm writing this piece. The phone rings. Afraid of losing my train of thought, I almost ignore it until I see that the caller is the caretaker of my cabin in the NC mountains. After we discuss mice, well water, and limbs that fell over the winter, I share Thoreau's famous thought on time. The caretaker responds that he lives out of sync with the way many people think of time. "Biology is a timer," he says. "It's a clock that winds down, but new studies are suggesting that you can influence the speed of biological time and reverse it. I don't think of aging as just trips around the sun."

These thoughts on time come from the mason who points chimneys, builds retaining walls, and checks kitchen drawers to make certain no snakes or mice nests are inside when I arrive in the spring. Conversations with him often inspire me to go deeper. Today, he delights in telling me that the grounds are abundant with juvenile American Toads. I've seen some of them myself, hopping the pathway or taking shade beneath Christmas ferns. In protected areas, some toads have been known to live forty years. But on the mountain, they live among predators.

He listens when I share Gibson's words about poetry. Then he continues: "A few days ago, walking to my truck, I heard a hummingbird but didn't see it. Instead of driving away, I lingered. I kept looking and listening."

"That's what Gibson is saying," I interject. "This is what poets do."

"Well, this is what I do with time. Even when working. Yesterday, I kept hearing the hummingbird. I stopped cleaning the gutters and climbed down the ladder. I followed the sound. I looked at a branch about twenty feet above my truck and saw the hummingbird. She was building a nest from tree lichens. Today, the bird was sitting inside the nest. I could barely see the top of her head. The beak was as thin as a needle."

"You took it in," I say.

"And maybe reversed a bit of my biological time!"

After the call, I read that hummingbirds are experts at camouflaging their nests. Photos of the nests shingled with lichen remind me of mosaic tiles. The nests are rare to spot— small bowls, tiny cups for the eggs.

Poems are containers of recollections, observations and more. We are often surprised by what they contain. Their layers bring new life to bear on our experiences, be they joyful, sorrowful or traumatic. Poetry provides hope. It helps us find our way.

Collage

Time is the stream I swim in.
I drink from it; and while I drink,
whatever takes my attention
I study it and take it home.

My gaze stirs the sand.
I fish the sky for what lies
beyond clouds and stars.
Some nights, I walk
the mountains of the moon.

One

During the Time of No Moon

Before dawn, follow the dog outside.
Stay awhile.

Listen to the birds practicing
melodies for the day.

Remember the time of kite-building
on the living room floor,

times you ran to the vacant lot next door
and sent messages up kite strings to the moon.

Lean into the wind, nimble as bamboo.
Hope has not abandoned you.

It nests among notes
you have written all your life.

Tucked into crevices,
ancient and gentle.

Reading Time

This morning he is an old poet wearing his blue shawl, hunched in the shade of the willow tree close to the nook of the pond, giving me pause to sit on the grass and watch until his blue wings open to the book of ages. How quietly the water wrinkles with lyrical lines floating to the surface, scrolling to shore from long ago.

O Basho, I think
of Wang Wei and cast my line
into the green pond

Indelible

O, word of choice,
you knew, of course,
which moments
I'd be remembering

~~~

Running free with the wind
in childhood down the middle
of dark streets in my
Westside neighborhood

~~~

Middle-aged
lost in the Dolomites
trusting the sense of smell
when darkness fell—

Scent of hay from the fields
my only compass
along the narrow trail
back to the farmhouse

Footsteps

after Victoria Chang

Sometimes   being   to   your
it takes   lost   find   self

Is   landscape   my   the
the   of   life   same

as   map   my
the   of   interior

If   could   out   my
I   step   of   body

would   foot   remain
my   prints   and

could   retrace
they   every

place   walked
I've   until

I   home
was

Pandemic Guests

although
the storm
and side-
blown rain
and gusts
of wind
threatened

uninvited
the guests
arrived
on the porch
tattered

they could
not know
what hope
they gave
before
they left

monarch
gecko
mantis

I Felt a Forest Growing in My Skin

I felt a forest growing in my skin
Rooted from all the places I had been
Then saw you crouched within a dream
The orchid mantis at the screen

The forest green within my skin
My arm outstretched at a neighbor's door
The pear plucked from a childhood tale
The paper wasp of memory

The paper wasp of memory
The pear plucked from a childhood tale
My arm outstretched at a neighbor's door
The forest green within my skin

The orchid mantis at the screen
You crouched within a dream
Rooted from all the places I had been
A forest grew within my skin

Talking to Siri in Pandemic Time

After my third or fourth nap, I asked Siri what time it was. She said she'd forgotten. I thought I was dreaming, so I asked again. This time she asked *Does time matter?* Siri, I said, **I'm** asking the questions. I want to know the time. And while you're calculating, let me know what day of the week it is. *Which day of the week?* she asked. I sat up in bed. Today! I shouted. What is today? *Today is a TV show*, she answered. I dangled my legs off the side of the bed. I'm not asking about TV, Siri. What is the freaking time? *Time is a band. Check Wiki. Time is a concept. You are living in pandemic time.* Siri, you don't need to remind me of that, I said, trying to control frustration. I'm simply asking, What is the time! *Which time?* she asked. *Pacific? Eastern?* Time for more coffee, I thought, as she continued. *Thyme is an herb. It is also the name of a magazine.* OK, OK, Siri. Listen. Let's try this. Silence. Had she disconnected? Hello, Siri, did you get that? *I'm pretty satisfied with what I've got.* Let's go back to thyme, the herb. Can I use it in Words with Friends? *I don't know*, she said. *I don't have friends.* This was becoming depressing. Siri, I can't go there with you. Honestly, I can see **WHY** you don't have friends, but I'm paying for you to give me the time of day. *I can't compute that*, she said.

Tea at My Potter Friend's *Wind Gather* Cabin, Jonas Ridge NC

I bring my own cup, teabag, hand sanitizer and wear a mask. She wears nitrile gloves when opening the bag of Pepperidge Farm cookies.

Heavy rainfall pounds the ground as we brace against the dampness, wearing wool sweaters on the porch, watching mists in the distance form layers that look like granite boulders.

We sip tea. Discuss how she shapes clay into images inspired by mountain musings, wraps them in foil and tucks them into the center of embers from the open fire she builds in her yard.

Her voice high-pitched with excitement, she speaks of rising early for coffee, throwing on her robe and rushing to the ashes to see the pots.

> *That's the beauty of it. The thrilling part. How the unknown shapes itself.*

Rejects are distractions. She piles them into cairns. Breaks them with a hammer. Tosses them into flower beds.

> *Quite a lovely sound that makes. Comforting, too, that it all returns to the earth. Nothing wasted. How is it with poetry?*

~~~

The mist lifts. We walk past a house—

once charming—bequeathed to children who never visit.

I touch a rusting chair. Feel the loneliness of windows—
curtains sagging—staring back at me. She points to the gutter
hanging from the porch.

A house untended doesn't keep itself up.

I secretly cringe when she reveals (and casually so) that a
possum enters her kitchen nightly through the cats' portal;
partakes of the cat food, then politely exits.

The cats don't mind. I think they rather like the night visitor.

Then there's the bear. The bear that scarred her car with
claws. The bear that left teeth marks on the trunk. Where is
that bear now?

We climb the backwoods trail. Pausing in the shade of an
oak, she confesses:

*At 84 I'm beginning to feel a bit old, but I don't tell everyone
that. So many don't know what a hike is. It's in the blood.
And the will to just carry on.*

Heron

at the pond

my dog and I

in willow shade

his nose

to earth

a few feet away

the Blue

in shallows

among reeds

beak a stiletto

plumage tight

a dark half-moon

waxing on his shoulder

before the wings'

unfolding

It Can Happen Anywhere

You glance through fence slats.
    Ghosts   move   like wind   in the field.

At the pond a silvery fin rises.
    Disappears   into   morning   mist.

Ants file across the sidewalk.
    Little   things   that   run   the   world.

A glossy mushroom
    glistens   in   the   grass.

Sunset churns voluminous clouds.
    Pockets   filled   with   mangoes.

In a small boat on the Han you drift,
    sip   wine   with   Wang Wei.

Praying Mantis on the Patio

Taking your time crossing the chair,
you slow my clock.
Where are you traveling, little one?
Why do you survive the virus
and a child does not?

Green prophet,
do you portend hope?
Forelegs folded, are you a monk
begging for your bowl?
Or an amputee lifting up a prayer?

Cold Long Night, 2020

Almost midnight. The clouds part.
The winter sky has never felt clearer.
The quaking stars never brighter.

I imagine the galaxy in concert:

    tubas   bells   flutes

performing for the stricken earth.

On this cold long night
nearing the end of December
the moon

peering between the maple's bare limbs—
a watchful eye
against the dark wall of sky.

Song for the Hours

O railroad spike—rusting in the field next to the splintered tracks I walked one summer alone into my father's past—I held you hot from the sun, heavy in my hand.

O train whistle of woe coming sure as nightfall to someone's porch. Opossum—cold by the roadside—your babies cling so tight to your nipples that the officer has to tug them loose before wrapping them into her handkerchief.

O mourning stars, have you lost your appointed place in the heavens?

O, Donne. Say it again: *Any man's death diminishes me.*

O, Mary Mallon (Typhoid Mary). Poor immigrant no one would miss. Creepy kudzu cannot smother the facts of your forced quarantine on North Brother Island.

O islands of respite and desolation.
    Pandemic islands. Hart Island.
    Islands choking on rough pavement.
    Islands of justice shot through with holes.

O, Abraham. Say it again: *Here I am.*

And here am I. Walking daily rounds in my courtyard, thinking of prisoners at recess tossing balls, jogging, puffing cigs. I pull weeds, inspect flowers, search for tender leaves, any rosebud; pause in sunlight to watch bumble bees suckle purple blossoms.

I think of those Alcatraz inmates who lovingly designed and landscaped gardens on that island. St. Francis of Assisi, in moments of loneliness and exile, withdrew to caves.

This morning's breeze tastes like freedom. The azure-colored wind spinner next to the iron swing goes wild, turning and turning.

I was once a child sitting on the city bus next to my mother, holding a windmill out the window. Joy coursed through my being, mingled with fumes from the streets.

Sweetness of bird song returns.

O wind chimes of my hours,

I am here.

Two

Sky Turtle

emerges
in the mackerel sky,
floating until it swallows
the flowering moon.
How bright that light
blossoming in its throat.

When You See a Shelf Mushroom

Note the artistry.
How it projects from trees—
a whimsical ledge
where insects may rest or shelter.
Note the humor.
How it sometimes loops
around broken limbs
resembling Pinocchio noses.
Praise its complexity.
Fluted like pie crusts & pizza slices
the shelf belies its toughness—
strong as wood you could carve.
It is a forbidden fruit in the garden
of fungi, doing what we all must
to survive.
Though the shelf rarely feasts
on living tissue, it can decompose
the heartwood of trees, gaining entry
through wounds caused by humans
carving initials, bears sharpening their claws,
a moose rubbing its antlers against bark.
Revel in the shelf's oxymoronic nature.
How it causes rot, yet heals—
offering herbals to the world,
recycling carbon,
playing many parts in the forest
of entrances and exits.

Salt

We lost touch somewhere in cyberspace,
lost the field of knowing where our lives were going.
So many fires raged, the world was mourning.
On the west coast a grandfather wept—
his house, wife, grandchildren burned to ashes
while ten minutes away he was shopping.
On the east coast the cardinal still came to the feeder.
Bluebirds nested in the house on the post.
A storm blew the fence into the neighbor's yard.
The dog went into surgery. Came home wearing
a red bandana. Wrapped in the silence
of the evening, I ate dinner. Sipped wine.
Pressed my fingertips to the white plate.
Licked the last grains of salt.

In the Sunlight of Enchantment

Today I took the dog out for pancakes.
Barking all the way he filled the car
with such joy I forgot my sorrow.

Forgot the fears of blood washing
into the Red Sea.

Forgot the news of women soldiers
   raped   dismembered   scattered.

Remembered instead a time when I sat
with a dear friend on the patio
at a private club in Mumbai.

Her daughter-in-law, an East Indian
doctor, ordered two bowls of sweet corn soup—
nourishment for

our bodies. Victims of a water-borne illness.
She pampered us. Drove us to the edge of
the Indian Ocean where we toasted our lives

sipping Merlot in the sunlight of enchantment.
I breathed deeply. Thought of inlets, even
buried ones, finding their ways home.

Remembered the map of the Red Sea I'd traced
in my childhood Bible. How I'd thought
if I ever saw it, the Sea would be the shade
of red I'd pulled from the Crayola box.

Maybe It Was Nott

We were standing close
to the curb trying to decide
which place to lunch
on a bustling street
in Chinatown.
Stockton, perhaps.
Years later I think
of it as Nott.
A cable car rattled past.
Then a man—
a huge net of frogs
slung across his back
I wished I hadn't seen.
Everything went silent.
The blaring horns.
The people cursing.
The sirens. The children crying.
The saxophone in the window.
No croaking from the net,
but I saw the terror
in their bulging eyes
and the stiff legs sticking
through the netting
as though they'd given up.
The man. The net. The frogs.
Their eyes. The legs.
They all disappeared in a flash.
Down an alley.
Behind a restaurant.

In the Dentist's Waiting Room, 2018

after Elizabeth Bishop

If Rockwell were painting this scene,
      I'd be the one sitting at the end of the floral sofa
            reading poems in old *New Yorker*s.

He'd paint the caretaker pushing
      an apple-red transport chair
            through the entrance.

But how could he capture the elderly woman
      in pink, gripping the arms and heaving
            heavy sighs into the silence

as she drops her feet
      (stuffed into Mary Janes)
            to the floor?

The man in blue jeans to my left
      looks on edge in the wingback chair,
            staring at the weather map

in the folded newspaper
      as if planning his day
            or perhaps a trip he doesn't want to take.

He finds reason to call or text,
      leaves the room,
            tapping his cell phone.

The day goes on raining.
       Bare trees lean
              against a grey sky.

To my right in a leather chair
       by the window
              a young man runs his fingers

through his scraggly hair. Only a whine
       disturbs the silence. He pats
              his comfort dog, its mouth clamped

inside a muzzle, leash strapped
       to the man's leg. The retriever looks bored,
              nose between paws.

Numbed by the poem I'm reading, I yawn
       and search the stack. Find outdated
              issues of *Our State* and *Garden & Gun*.

Glancing sideways I note that the woman
       in pink seems frozen in a semblance of herself,
              mouth wide open. Not even a snore snaps

her awake. I wait, but nothing happens.
       Her caretaker lost, too, somewhere inside
              ear buds plugged into a white iPod.

Rockwell's brush tilts back to me
       unmoored on the couch
              waiting for my porcelain crown.

The Roofers

The crews arrived early this morning.
Standing across the street from my house,
I am drawn to the woman astride
the arch of my roof.

Wind lifts her blonde dreadlocks.
Strutting against a backdrop of blue sky
and billowing clouds, she is a goddess-rapper

shouting instructions, dancing across the roof
to the music of scrapers, staplers,
hammers, shingles flung to the ground,

ripped tarps flapping, the wind whistling
through the gaps, men yelling:
Don't throw that box! Look!
That woman's walking her dog again.

They break into song. At lunchtime,
plug cookers into porch outlets.
Fry fajitas   tortillas   tacos.

The neighborhood feels festive.
Something new:
Aromas spiced with singing
flowing freely through the streets.

I walk the dog round and round the block.
Hungry myself for something
bright and unforeseen on the horizon.

I Drive Old Monroe Road

The view that cuts the heart chokes the soul.
The eye cannot behold it all at once.
Trees that once lined driveways for
decades reduced to jagged stumps.
Mile after mile, amputated oaks standing
as if in assembly lines awaiting executions.
Sacrifices for the future Super Street.

The sprawling white farmhouse looks forlorn
as if, overnight, robbed of its tranquility.
A family cemetery, an ice house, rusted tractor
scaled with kudzu, the well house nailed shut—
all exposed in fields where horses plowed
and honeybees settled when night fell.

Through the seasons I've photographed
this farm that tugged at some sense of kinship.
Christmas times, I've lowered the car window
and meditated on the stars shimmering
above the rooster weather vane.
In time, those stars will recede.

A dirge drifts in the air:

> Voices of winds—
> susurrous—
> as though traveling
> in the presence
> of leaves
> murmurous

Milkweed, Jonas Ridge NC

That spring she planted milkweed across the road from
Cozie Cottage on Bald Mountain. It was 2008. Thought
she was doing it for the butterflies.

By 2010 the milkweed had spread across the field, reaching
the apple trees. During the Great Migration, waves of
Monarchs followed invisible scents

to her place. Spent several splendid nights. Imagine ecstasy.
Plentiful drumming, feeding, laying of eggs.

Before they left, Susan drove her mother through
the wonder of it all—

Grandfather Mountain watching in the distance.
In 2014 her mother, at 96, took flight.

Though the milkweed has thinned and moved down
the slope, it remains a plant of hope. 2024.

For the Monarch. The earth.
And for the memories it sows.

Three

Remembering Linda Pastan

After a friend calls and says she's just
heard an outpouring of affection and
grief from your fans on social media,
I search obituaries in the *NYT*.

But what pops up on the screen
is your poem "My Obituary" as if
you've become a ghost writer
in the afterlife, your persistent
dry humor breaking through cyberspace
making me remember your broad smile,
the glint in your bluest of eyes
when I photographed you at the door
of the guest house on Sardis Road
before your morning talk
and you told me lady bugs had infested
your toothbrush overnight.

Though I scroll compulsively
for an official notice, it isn't there.

I can almost hear you saying:

> It's true this time, not a metaphor.
> Death was always hiding
> along every path I walked. Even
> behind the oaks and poplars,
> the ironwood and dogwood
> in my acres of woods.

Titles and words, as I thumb
through your books,
transform into dark gloves
waving farewell.
A scroll that won't stop.

I sit by the window,
the dog lying on the floor,
his head resting on my feet.

For a long time, we stay
this way—
watching the icy rain
and the wind-whipped maple,

its last leaves holding
until stems break free.
...*the simple act*
of turning and walking away
feels forbidden
this frozen day.

Collage for a Friend in Grief

Even in childhood she seemed to know
each loss introduces us step by step
to death's domain.
I am writing here of Glück.

Life ends—though broken relationships,
tended in memory, live on. Can heal.
He never sang for his father.
I am speaking here of Anderson.

Then, there's Hirsch. Going blind. Still,
capturing moments he never thought of
as indelible until the time came when
he would. Over years. The losses.
He remembers how the sun spangled
the trees one autumn day. The radiance.

Song for the Sea Lion, Steep Ravine CA

June. The waves of the Pacific recede, having delivered their early-morning gifts. Among them, spread out like a golden shroud upon the rocks beneath the cliffs, lies the Sea Lion.

Somber as the clouds thundering over Stinson Beach, my 12-year-old niece Monica and I climb down toward the tidal pools, holding our breaths against the stench in the wind. Vultures—black-cloaked judges lined up in a row on fragile hilltops—watch intently.

~~~

The mother sea lion bleeds a thin stream over the rocks and into the coarse sand. The surf weaves a white wreath around her. We pace, our gaze fixed on her eye sockets where black flies buzz. We shiver at the exposed brain. The vultures, now indifferent witnesses, pluck their shiny feathers. They know how to wait.

~~~

Still, even in death. Even in *this* death. Something holy must be present. For how sweet, how demure her face with sunlight glancing off the stiff whiskers. How the whiskers sparkle.

~~~

Several pups sun in the sand by the ocean's edge perhaps learning to survive alone. And we who are staring at the wound near a mother's heart—what are we waiting for? Caught in the mystery of what happened here. The wind shifts. We think we hear a song coming *from some symphonic distance.*

~~~

At night in the cabin. In a dream, the soft cry of a lost sea pup. An aria from the beating heart. The tiny beacon of its body shimmers in moonlight as it struggles up a boulder, clapping its fins in desperation. Its silken skin is scarred with stars. It lumbers down the rocks. It reenters the belly of the ocean.

~~~

At dawn, Monica and I return to the tidal pool near the shore. The pups are gone. The vultures perched on the bluff watch our descent. The blood on the rocks has darkened. We approach the sea lion for one last look, our hands offering what might be a prayer.

Remembering Miroslav Holub *from Some Symphonic Distance*

The pendulum on the grandmother clock
has slowed in my home on the east coast
and the iron mantle clock has stopped ticking.

Vultures around the world circle
forever searching
coasts, boulders, mountains.
They know how to wait their turn.

And Death will always arrive
carrying its tattered calendar.

The story goes that on an ordinary
day in July *from some symphonic distance*
unexpectedly
it stepped to the door of your home
near Prague.

Perhaps you were shaving.

And the fairy tale you fashioned
found an ending.

The Seal Skin woman
slipped back into the sea
and swims there still
listening to the *song of the whales*
that contain you.
And you—in the *genetic background*—
begin anew.

Legacy, 2020

for Barry Lopez, January 6, 1945 – December 25, 2020

> *His hunger to understand the roots of cruelty*
> *was located in his wounds.*
>
> ~Terry Tempest Williams

Many stories will rise
from the ashes
of the McKenzie fire,
destroyer of his
50-year-old archives.

His wife will tell
how weeks later
in dense smoky air
he sifted through ashes,
grasping lines he had typed.
Watched the words crumble
in his hands.

Stories will lament
how it burned
into his soul—his body
already stricken by cancer.

And some will say
he went stumbling
like a mad man
through acres of trees,
picking up limbs
smoldering in rain.

More than one
will paint him kneeling
by the ever-changing river.
The way he waded into it.
Weeping.

Four

Another Wandering Aengus

The day packs up its bags
and slowly leaves

as another wandering Aengus
roams the fields and woods

as half-light casts its spell
and dusky shades are drawn
so dreams may come.

Nocturnal voices begin
their stridulations

of ancient songs
that never left the earth.

The moths. The moon.
The echolocation.
The orientation of stars.

The flutter. The flicker.
The swelling of the ground.

Luminescent:
Fairy fire in the wood—

You Entered My Car Years Later

You entered my car years later
when Schubert's "Trout" Quintet was playing
as if there'd be no ending,
the piano picking up where we'd left off.
Oh, how I love the "Trout," you said.
We sat in silence, listening,
the way we used to in the dorm.
The look on your face was ethereal,
the same as when you watched ballet
or heard Beethoven's 7th—the Allegretto.
On one of my Chopin albums, you wrote:
    This moment is the best the world can give.
And here we were again
as if there'd been no ending—
the melody pulsing
beneath Serkin's fingers
and all those trout swimming.

The Rug

in memory of Gloria Cooper

Luscious, the sheepskin rug beneath my feet.
Such a lavish gift, you downplayed it.
Pressed the plush pile to your cheeks:

> *Do what you want with it.*
> *Toss it over a chair for flair.*
> *Or throw it on the floor.*
> *Maybe it'll keep you warm*
> *some time.*

Two months later, you dozed in a hospice house,
a crocheted prayer blanket at your feet.

You must have sensed there'd come a day
when I'd understand that feet, too, need comfort.
We should spoil them. Try to remember
what they've stood for or on. Where
they've traveled. The blisters they've endured.
The agony of pointe work.
You in *Swan Lake*.

Without Feathers

Returning to my car, I photograph the green bike
parked in a tight corner between a broken fence
and stacks of cardboard boxes, a sign reading
"Waterfowl Rescue" wired to the rear basket.

A little town in America, fifteen miles from my home
where, this morning, my dog barked so persistently
that I closed the book I was reading, followed his bark
to the hatchling upside down on the ground beneath
the cedar tree, chirping frantically, naked body
twisting in 100-degree heat.

In an unsettled world how small this tiny tragedy.
Did it matter that the father cardinal flew close?
A streak of red like a warning flag? A signal for help?
Did it matter that I lined a shoe box with wet
paper towels to cool the tiny body?

How quiet the drive to Poplin Road.
Not a peep from the box.
Did it matter that traffic was heavy?
That I was delivering a newborn
Mother Nature herself had blown from the nest?

Taped to the wooden door, a sign:
Short of staff. Welcome! Come inside.
A shack of a place where, out of the cloud of dust
and clutter, a volunteer appeared—a manifestation
of St. Teresa—her smile radiating all the love
this moment needed.

Talisman

Greek telein: *"to initiate into the mysteries"*

This white stone I hold
Found in Mykonos

Round as a biscuit
It feeds me

In my palm
Held up to the sky

It becomes a full moon

O

Round as a biscuit
It becomes a full moon

Held to the sky
By my hand

It feeds me

This white stone I hold
Found in Mykonos

O

Held to the sky
By my hand

It becomes a full moon
Round as a biscuit

This white stone I hold
Found in Mykonos
It feeds me

O

Easter, and the pear trees blossom

followed by the cherry and
soon the redbud

which blooms first
doesn't matter for

in Amsterdam
almond blossoms are always

climbing the limbs
on Van Gogh's canvas

the red rose pinned to my blouse
before church smells sweet again

but the white one my childhood friend
wears is turning brown

Mother's Day tinges with sadness
now that the dogwood's twisted

branches bear white leaves
bracts to ease the pain

Ashes

in memory of Helen Stroupe

We've divided her ashes,
such is our cultural divide.

Friends in the spirit of children
carry small sacks to the sea.

Others circle her cabin.
Some hike through rhododendron

up to Sitting Bear Rock and
along Gingercake Road.

Think of Chinese lanterns
lighting mountain trails.

Think of fireflies.
I predict deep snows

on Jonas Ridge
come December.

And next summer, foxfire
like stars in the ditches.

Beginning an Elegy

for Margaret

as the heart grows older ... you will weep and know why
~Gerard Manley Hopkins

There are intervals, after all, that last.
An awareness that never departs.
Because. It runs deep. Like.
A silent announcement you alone
heard. A chord rang inside you.
A taut violin string trembled.
And you knew you were in the presence
of something you could not name.

✦

On one of many nights on a college campus
an English professor walked her student
to the dorm.
They stopped beneath a soft yellow lamplight,
the fog settling, giving the evening the feel of
a Hardy poem.

During their walk the teacher had spoken of vessels—
their different sizes, capacities—relating that
to compassion, trying to help her student
better understand Chekhov's "Lament":

How the old cabman whose son has died
reaches out and is met with vacuousness.
No one listens or cares about his grief.
Back at the stables, he brushes his horse.
Whispers his sorrow into his ear.

The teacher knew that the student's mother,
an alcoholic, had phoned that day. Suicidal.
Before they parted, she pulled the black
velvet collar of her coat closer to her neck
and said, "I've never had a relationship
like this with a student. If I can help …
I'll be anything you want me to be."

The lamplight. The fog. The aura.
The alluring ambiguity contained within
one sentence flew directly to the heart.
They never spoke of it again.

Whether they sat on stone benches
outside the library or took long walks
to the pond. Whether in her office
they discussed literature, sorrows,
and life's mounting uncertainties,
the teacher weighed her words.
Consoler. Mentor. Confidante.

All this was a long time ago.

Sometimes on their walks
they heard strains of concertos
(Chopin and Rachmaninoff)
floating from the "practice shacks"
where students prepared for concerts.
This, too, became part of them at sundown.
They sat beneath oaks. Tried to imagine
Blake's host of angels on the boughs.

She laughed when the student,
spying a praying mantis prone
on a blade of grass, mimicked Wordsworth:
>   *Up! Up! ... Let Nature be your teacher.*
"Only you," she said.
Some nights the student slipped poems
under her office door.
Some nights she turned away.

On days when the class was writing
final exams in blue books
and the teacher monitored, strolling the rows,
her scent of lavender lingered over words
the student penned to blue lines on the page,
staying within the margins,
trying to capture the images
her fierce mentor had stirred to life.

A Way into the Trees

Today we celebrated
the *loveliest of trees*
and sat beneath
the cherry's boughs
reading Housman
aloud   then reciting
his poem by heart—
close friends in the flux
of juxtapositions.
If relief came
we did not say
when we parted
though I felt
we'd stored gladness
in the house
inside ourselves
having pushed aside
the busyness
that taxed our lives
as we found a way
into the trees
already spending
their

b

  r

i

     e   f   f l

               u r

                  r y

Five

Words

When Bob Hass reads from his manuscript at Squaw Valley, some of the pages drift to the floor and rest next to the lectern. He seems not to notice. Not to care. Then borrows someone's reading glasses. Says he knew one day this would happen. The glasses make things worse. He laughs and holds the Milosz book at arm's length in dim light. The words scattered on the floor become jealous. Especially the page he steps on now as he intones Seamus Heaney. The words crawl off the page, away from his feet. And when he shifts and recites from his heart his own poem, the words on the floor turn into *muskrats* and *black-eyed Susans* and *ponds. You can go into that meadow…. You can go there.* His reading ends. Amid applause, he reaches down, gathers the pages from the floor as if picking wild flowers, tries shuffling them into a bouquet. The words are prickly as briars. He keeps calling them back as if calling to something in the *blue-gray distance.* The words obey. And the words that never were there on those pages are listening at the windows.

Poetry Reading at an Indian Trail Cafe

The place was closed when poets arrived at seven.
The moderator leaned into my car window,
said he hadn't heard a thing.
A cardboard clock read "back at 8."
Then we saw the sign: For Sale.
Cars and vans began circling the lot,
drivers asking, "Where's the reading?"
"Supposed to be here," the moderator said.
The entire strip was closed.
"Let's wait fifteen minutes."
Some drove down the road for gas.
Scheduled poets, eager to read, waited,
among them an editor and a Presbyterian minister.

The amazing part is that the young folks stayed,
sitting in pickup trucks and tired vans,
holding babies or standing in clusters, talking
softly among hopefuls holding sheaves of poems
for the Open Mic.
"Let's do it!" someone called.
We all backed our vehicles to the sidewalk
and held a tailgate reading in front of the cafe—
poets standing behind a wrought iron hand rail,
babies sitting quietly in strollers,
mamas and papas nodding in unison to rhythms
of poems. Asking how much our books cost.

"I loved your poetry and will follow anywhere
you read," a teenager said, handing me his email
address. That was payment enough.
Said he had ADHD, kept his poems short
so he'd remember what he was writing.
"Good advice for us all," I replied.

During the Open Mic, I sat on someone's camp
stool. Remembered a friend's trip to Haiti.
Students with no electricity in their homes
sat on curbs, studying beneath street lights.
Here, at the sweetest reading I'd ever attended,
poets read under purple and yellow neon lights,
feeling heat on their necks,
and the hungry waited to be fed.

Cicada, I Never Knew You Were the Loudest Insect in the World Until I Read

that you are not born to solitude
but seek a chorus that sings in decibels
sometimes louder than a rock concert.
That in folklore your singing signaled
six weeks till frost and summer's ending.

Today, I discovered your exoskeleton
clinging upside down to my fence.
I pried it loose. Held it in my palm.

Until today I had never noticed
the slit in the carcass.
Never before thought of us as kin,
of what enormous energy it took
for you to burst through—
birthing yourself.
Never considered the possibility
of your pain.
Never dreamed your ribs
were buckling and snapping
hundreds of times per second.

Just as family members
have their own stories to tell,
each of your species thrums
a different song.

I underestimated you, Cicada,
listening to your whirls of music,
never a distraction—
more a calling to pause,
lie down in the fields.

Leaves, Curbside

The yellow school bus barrels past.
Its stop sign swings out.
A stiff arm swatting the air.
Cars brake. Kids jabber walk.
Backs laden with book packs.
Two fourth-grade boys
who love my puppy
leap into mounds of leaves
the landscapers blew to the curb.
I used to do that. What fun! I say
when the boys rush to pat Tanner.

We chat about the possum
I saw in my yard last night.
A rare white one. *A good omen,*
I tell them.
Do you know how to play dead?
"That was an albino," Jacob says.
"Possums play dead to save themselves."
Steve adds that his granddaddy plays dead.
"He's on oxygen."

The next day more piles
of leaves line the roadsides.
Swollen and silent as fresh graves.
Except for two—the ones with deep
impressions where children play dead.

Email Morning

I don't want to see another photo
of the albino moose, another email
ornament luring me away from finishing
the novel I'm reading or searching
for receipts for Uncle Sam.
I don't want to open another warning
about cocoa mulch that kills pets
or read another alarm about microwaved
hot water blowing up in a man's face.
Not even the tea bag is safe.
I scan poems from *The Writer's Almanac*.
Scroll to the last lines of Jim Harrison's
"Cold Poem" where the poem
blows its nose and declares:
    time drifts past you like the gentlest,
    almost imperceptible breeze.
It troubles me—that part about the breeze—
enough to make me click on "Save" and sneeze.

Octopus Farming for the Food Harvest

Imagine hundreds of intelligent sentient octopi
stuffed into small tanks, freezing until they die.

Promising no longer to partake
of this cephalopod family,
I confess to having relished
their taste on a balcony
overlooking Cephalonia's cliffs
and the Ionian Sea

(and many times elsewhere
    before & thereafter)

though
none with the ambience
of being in Greece—
Robola wines,
exuberant conversations at once
among friends seated close
to potted lemon trees,
fuchsia bougainvillea leaning
over walls—

so
I donate this edible poem
to readers who may or may not
understand the choice,
entangled as we all are
in word-tanks
during dangerous times.

One Peppermint Ball

This is the first time Mama has trusted me
to walk alone to the grocery at the end of our street.
The grocer and his family live upstairs.

The old woman knitting in the rocker
in the dark store hunches toward the window
to catch the sunlight. Her hair is knotted
into a tight wad that looks like a grenade.
She doesn't even glance up when I enter.
I could be a five-year-old ghost.

The grocer towers over the countertop.
I hand him the wrinkled list.
He moves to the meat counter and begins
slicing olive loaf for Daddy's sandwiches.
My eyes roam the delicacies
in jars, wicker baskets, cardboard boxes.
Dubble Bubble. Licorice. Hershey bars.

The old woman's rocking makes the floor tremble.
Her knitting needles click like granddaddy's teeth.
The long minute hand of the clock on the wall
seems to move faster as my heart races.
She would be bent over, I'm thinking, squinting
at each stitch. I grab a peppermint.
Pop it into my mouth. It's so creamy soft
it'll melt quickly. No one will know.

The grocer plops the lunch meat wrapped
in thick butchers' paper onto the counter,
announcing each item as he presses
the machine's keys and cranks out numbers:
one pound of butter, a half-pound of olive loaf,
quarter pound of Swiss cheese. Will that be all?
Before I can say *yes, sir*
a creaky voice chills my spine:
    add one peppermint ball.

She didn't miss a stitch.
Just kept rocking as I headed out the door,
cheeks burning.

When the Challenge Came in Fifth Grade

to meet the girl bully at the corner lot after school for a fight, I felt like a piñata hit so hard by a peppermint candy cane that all the confetti laughed its way down the sidewalk, exposing every secret I'd carried my entire life. With friends walking behind me, I thought of the movie "High Noon," the theme song playing in my head as I marched, thinking Gary Cooper didn't look afraid but he was a man—not a ten-year-old girl who didn't want to be a sheriff anyway. I knew I'd lose, but didn't let on.

When we arrived at the vacant lot behind Woodstock Baptist Church, I regretted that the pastor didn't run out & chase us away. We waited a long time, stirring the gravel with the toes of our black & white Oxfords. After what seemed like hours, a friend raised my arm & pronounced me Champion of the Fighting Lot, won by default because She-Bully never showed. I didn't want that title. Was relieved I could go home without a black eye.

~~~

As for piñatas. They remain a mystery.
I've never whacked one.
But the myth of the piñata filled with hosts
of fears remained with me well into adulthood.
Decades would pass before I'd learn:
There is no illusion greater than fear.

Ten Years Old and She No Longer Believes in Santa

You no longer believe? I asked,
needing to know because she'll be spending
a week with me this Christmas.

"He's not real, Aunt Irene. You've carried your life
this far and don't know that?"

Well, how can you be so sure?

"He told me so. On the phone.
I'm his favorite kid in Hortense.
He wouldn't lie to me."

If you were on the phone with him, he was real.

"He's here now. When he takes his hat off,
he disappears."

Back to the North Pole, I say. Where his elves
work all year round.

"Don't forget. Leave some limbs bare on the tree
so I can hang ornaments.
I called Discovery Place this morning and asked
the man if that dinosaur they had trapped
in the crate last summer was still there.
It's gone! He said too many kids were scared of it."

You actually called Discovery Place?

"Yep. So can we go to the Bug Exhibit
if it doesn't cost too much?"

Of course. I just want to be sure.
You really believe the dinosaur's gone?

"Yep. Just in case Santa's real,
do you think he knows I'll be coming up there?"

Absolutely, I say. And we'll have Cornish hens
on Christmas Eve.

"What's a Cornish hen?"

Something very special. Like you.

Joy

after Mary Szybist

I had the happy idea I could be eating breakfast at my
    friend's table in California and become bees pollinating
    her roses.

Over oatmeal and blueberries, I saw the Lafayette hills mixed
    with shadow and light reflected in the patio window.

I had the happy idea I could enter the reflection and begin
    hiking the path to the eucalyptus trees.

Sitting in the gravity chair on the deck, I imagined myself
    a passenger on a jet, flying *East of Eden* on a *Long Day's
    Journey into Night*.

I had the happy idea I could be both the seashell sunning in
    a Peruvian basket and hot-pink geraniums soaking up
    water in terra-cotta pots.

I had the happy idea I could become Jarrell's bat-poet, hitch
    a ride on a red-shouldered hawk, write a poem while
    hovering above the witch's house after Gretel pushes her
    into the oven.

I had the happy idea apples and walnuts and pomegranates
   could mingle. A host of flavors and fragrances never
   before tasted or smelled would be born.

My happiest wish was that the ocean would wash over my
   skin and purify the life within my body. The marrow
   of my bones, the tissue beneath my skull, would all be
   renewed.

And if I truly imagined myself as happy, the pines with
   candle-like candelabras would light up each night. No
   one would even try to explain mystery.

Six

Moon

Though some have
called you *corpse*
you are alive to me
no matter how
ghostly you appear
early mornings
the sky gauzy

When the Last Page Turns

When the last page turns

will I step into a star

on a moonless night

or drift deep into the dark

maybe alight on your door screen

a firefly—a single green lantern?

Wherever I was when last

you read me

let the empty space

remember

Each Morning, the Fall

Each morning, the fall more colorful,
though heaviness lingers like an evening fog.
Streams of sunlight burn through the window.
From the cabin door I watch autumn
leaves dance, play tiny tunes with the wind.
I lift the Kalimba from the wall. Its music cuts.
My heart won't play. It is a string-less lute.
Last week I wrapped you in your soft green
blanket. Did not want you cold on that
metal table. Held you in my lap when the
vet gave the sedative that would take you
away from me. My hand felt your last heartbeat.
She left us alone. I cut a lock of your fur.
Placed your first toy (the blue doggie now
16 years old) beside your face.
Drove home, thinking of the trust, the love.
That last joyful gaze.

in memory of Boscoe

A Dream That Still Makes Me Cry

The hardwood floors are covered with dried
twigs and crusty leaves.
My brother pushes an oversized vacuum, bag
blown tight as a balloon.
Better use a broom now. This thing is overheating.

He begins sweeping.
I pull dog toys and dust bunnies from beneath
the lounger.
My elbow hits his ankle.
I'm sorry he says as if he's done something wrong.
Not your fault, I say.

He slumps onto the couch, puts his hands
behind his head. His arms spread like bat wings.
He is wearing faded jeans and a blue sweatshirt
with a logo in black lettering like the one he wore
on his last visit.

This will be the last time, he says.
Why? I ask, afraid he is offended by something,
won't return.
*It's an easy trip back   just up the highway
a quick turn   toward Jacksonville
the rest of the way   through swamp.*

Why, among My Brothers

Why, among my brothers,
do I think of you more often
than I do the other two
who stand in the shadows
in the other world?

Please, don't be jealous, I say
to the other two.
He, the oldest, was
the last to leave and
took our childhood with him.

The Dead Don't Miss Us

That's what some say,
but who are *they* anyway—
those who make such pronouncements.

Hard to believe you don't miss me
opening a can of oysters and stirring them
till they wrinkled in a pot of steaming milk.
And how we crumbled saltines into the bowl,
drank the stew down to the flecks
of black pepper.

Surely, you miss our sitting beside each other
at the county auction, not bidding on anything
or betting on who'd live the longest.
And that time you took me for a ride
on your squatty motor scooter.
I felt so proud you'd paid attention:
you, a teenager; me, a sixth grader.

No, I don't believe those who say
the dead don't miss us.
You told me so yourself,
days before you died:
I hang on because I'm going to miss you.
Until that moment I'd never thought about it.
Lost, I was, clinging to memories we were making.

The other day I caught a glimpse of you
moving from behind me to the living room,
wearing the red plaid jacket you'd worn at my cabin.
Such an odd time for you to show up.
Just when I'm pouring detergent into the washer.
But, then, I remembered how on school days
we sometimes scrubbed our dirty socks
in the bathroom sink and spread them
on top of the oil heater to dry overnight.
Maybe it's times like that—the mundane—
you miss most.

The House within a Mansion

My parents and my younger brother Ronnie and I are on a house tour, walking over grassy terrain. Ronnie points to the address: 2584. We are astonished. The tour guide, never visible, is only a Voice, yet a presence we feel as we enter a brick mansion. Our house was not made of brick. One year the wood siding was covered with Perma stone. So why does this mansion have our address?

It is magnificent, not the two-bedroom bungalow built in 1938. We enter a foyer and stare way up to the ceiling which is framed by gold molding. A mural of godly and angelic figures like something from the Sistine Chapel hovers over us. Too majestic for our humble furnishings. If we lived here, how could I ever say again that at times we were close to poor—at least it felt that way. Just as feeling at home here seems real, yet unreal. My older brother Ralph once explained to me that we weren't ever poor by socio-economic standards. He said our family was lower working class.

The Voice tells us to keep moving into the foyer. Daddy smiles as he recognizes his handiwork. He installed the small domino-shaped pieces in our bathroom the year I was born. I loved those white tiles with a black cube in the center. They look out of place in this gigantic foyer. How amazed we are that the tile is so well preserved.

Moving quickly from room to room, we sense the wooden structure of our home. Looking through a window, I see the back door and the three concrete steps that led to the back yard. *Look,* I say to Ronnie. *Our back stoop is attached to this place. Ralph and I sat on those steps. Cracked coconut shells with Daddy's hammer. Sometimes we nailed through the three coconut eyes and drank the sweet water.*

The guide moves everyone into the living room. Ronnie says, *And, look! There's the rug.* Mama loves that rug. It is long and rose colored, richly faded. I lift a corner to look for a label. The rug is not heavy, though. It feels like a crocheted rug. If I roll it up, can I take it with me without anyone noticing?

The Voice hurries us along. We come to a table with items for sale. Are these from our house? Souvenirs of the tour? I lift a blue enameled dish pan which someone has made into a lamp. A price tag dangles from the cord. Can I afford it? Ronnie says, *It's only $7.49.* Before I can buy it, the tour ends abruptly.

The sky turns gray. Oh, how we hate leaving. We have loved being together again. The living and the departed. Family. Inside our old house on Lowell. Within a mansion. Within a dream.

Landlines and Train Tracks

We were talking on our landlines,
my brother and I, long-distanced.

I could picture him rocking
alone in his small apartment,

a train whistling far away in the night
entering the lines without warning,

imposing a silence on our words—
the engine splitting the darkness

like the shock of wood
when a cold axe strikes the core.

Every night, he said, *when the train
rumbles through*, I think of Dad.

Those tracks took us to other places—
kids, again, standing on a caboose.

Exuberant in strong winds.
Unaware we were watching life flying past.

Adobe House, Taos

In the adobe house I'd rented one summer, I placed an orange inside a small wall niche in memory of my father. It glowed like a candle on an altar.

The next day I found a blue feather on the path. That night I took it from my pocket and leaned it against the wall in the alcove. Its shadow fluttered like the jay's wing.

The next morning, I drove to Ranchos de Taos, stood on a scaffold, plunged bare hands into a bucket of mud. At ease among villagers who sang as we re-mudded the walls of San Francisco de Asis.

Before leaving, I pulled the rope dangling from the bell tower. The blue sky swelled with music. The whole day felt like a prayer.

That night I took a mud rock from my pocket and put it in the wall-cave.

In the morning, the orange was still glowing. The shadow of the feather had flown. The straw in the mud rock glittered like gold.

The walls hummed like bees among flowers when I dropped the key to the table. Drumming and chanting filled the streets.

I drove away, heading home.

Mama was Clever

The day she read the letter
stating I couldn't begin first grade
until I was six,
she poked a hole
in my birth certificate
with a rusty nail.
On enrollment day
she handed it to the principal
who asked, "What happened
to your daughter's birth date?"
Mama apologized,
said she kept important
papers on a nail
in the bedroom closet,
hadn't meant to punch out
the year I was born.
The principal held
the certificate to the sunlight,
rubbed her forefinger
over the piercing,
while I stood like
a tin soldier at Mama's side,
the certificate reminding me
of one of those punch cards
you could poke at the corner store
for a nickel.
If you were lucky
you'd win a prize.
Mama won.

The principal smiled
down at me
and I grew much
older than I was.

Ars Poetica

the

poem

that

swims

to

the

ocean's

depths

discovers

holes

it

can

not

fill

and

notes

it

can

not

take

Beyond the Iron Gate

After all these years
I feel it
The overwhelm of grief
Covering your grave
Parched in clay
Drawing me
Out of the shade

I go to meet it
Carrying grief
Buzzards on alert
Worm moon rising

Are you safe now
I want to ask
Kneeling
Did you know
I sang you a lullaby
The night you were dying

Worm moon rising
Buzzards on alert
Carrying grief
I go to meet it

Out of the shade
Drawing me

Parched in clay
Covering your grave
The overwhelm of grief

I feel it
After all these years

I Asked Rilke's Darkest Angels

Wrap wings around me.
Straighten my back.

Soothe my fears
with your rough feathers.

Guard the door
where light seeps through.

Sweep the glass
from the sidewalk.

Uproot the storm's damaged rosemary.
Haul it away in a funereal truck.

I invited those angels:
Move in and stay.

Blow out the *guttering candle*
in the *deep unknown*.

They covered their faces
in sorrow. Backed away.

I watched them through venetian blinds
perch on the fence beside the peregrine.

There they wait in a *sheen of light*.

Seven

What's past is prologue.
Shakespeare, *The Tempest*

What follows is a dramatic poem, structurally inspired by ancient Greek techniques and by T. S. Eliot's *Choruses from the Rock*. It is a mode I chose in one of many attempts to understand the tragedy of my mother's life. Composed of many voices—human and nonhuman—the poem begins with the collective pronoun "we." I invite readers to take a leap of imagination and become part of the "we," entering a deep forest and coming upon an outdoor assembly.

We Came to a Place that was Grieving and Gathered to Listen

CHORUS:

We gather to listen
that the wounded may be healed.
Without stories we lose our way.
What is forgotten will be remembered.
What is buried, unearthed.
Let the litany begin.

ECHOES OF VOICES:

I was the minister preaching redemption.
I was the no-see-um in the pulpit.
I was the mantis preying in the offering plate.
I was the genealogy a mother burned in the garden.
I, the black snake, watched from her washshed.

CHORUS:

There is a time for all to speak.
A time for all to listen.

LADY LUCK:

I, Lady Luck, for years sat in the church
pews, until one day, weary of our liaisons,
I shot the preacher dead.

He dropped like a duck on my lawn.
I was ruled insane, locked away.
So many stories left untold.

MOTHER:

Shall I begin my own litany of doom?
What came after? What went before?

Once I was a leader in that church.
My husband, a deacon.
Finest man I ever knew.
We entertained speakers in our home.
I taught Sunday School. Canned
tomatoes in the church kitchen.

CHORUS:

We have heard it said
this was not enough.
She craved more.
Each life hungers
for its own experience.

MOTHER:

I ran away from the farm.
Had little education except
in the fields. Married.
Bore children. Sold Avon.
Served appetizers

at Daylight Groceries.
Delivered politicians' pamphlets.
Babysat for doctors' families.
Until....

Oh,
I ramble in this résumé of ruin.
My children. They remember
I tried.
Once, a hurricane blew the glass
from the bedroom window.
I sat between them on the bed.
The Bible open in my lap.
And prayed.

A few years later at church one night
I wrapped my arms around their shoulders.
Walked between them down the aisle.
Wanted to save them.

Lady Luck's minister (and mine)
welcomed them into the fold.
He came to our house, too.
As did a friend's husband.
Something cracked inside
my heart. The center
did not hold.

I became Lady Icarus draped
over the clothesline
by wagging tongues.

CHORUS:

More than illusion.
More than delusion.
Something other than.
Something deeper than confusion.

MOTHER:

Oh, do not ask what happened.
The good Lord knows.
My daughter asked me once,
sitting next to me on the porch swing,
if I could help her understand.
All I could think to say was:
Loneliness.

People with loose lips blamed my demise,
my fall from the church—my scorn of it—
my agony and crazed state,
on the change of life.
A psychiatrist found my jokes amusing.

Nothing wrong with her, he said,

returning me to my family waiting
in the lobby. At my own peril
I had become a Master Illusionist.
A Jester even he could not see drowning.

CHORUS:

The Muses say Penelope paced.
Behind her loom wove her web.
Yet, could not unravel her place.
When the men went to battle,
she dreamed of pet geese.
Wept that her voice was lost.

MOTHER:

I will not defile this space.
Will not utter here all I said and did.
What I became   other than this:

    I became Lady Arsonist.
    Burned the Bible in the backyard.
    I became Madam Fury, fanning the flames.
    I became Lady Divinity in the kitchen by day.
    Lady Wino in the closet by night.
    I became Lady Bagworm
    dragging my home through the streets.
    To my children and their father
    I became the ghost that never died.

EHOES OF VOICES:

We, the humming birds she fed, tallied her visits.
We, the bees, pollinating flowers, recognized her face.
We, the willows, wept with her when she stretched out on
our roots.

DAUGHTER:

Sometimes she comes as chimes on the wind.
Becomes choruses of frogs in swamp lands.
Sometimes she reaches for blushing lilies.
Sometimes floats on buoyant leaves.
She becomes spoonbills stepping into cool waters.
Becomes ghost beads rattling inside Peruvian shakers.
Becomes a mouse poised in an alley.
Becomes trees whispering secrets to nameless stones.

MOTHER:

My daughter,

When you thought you were lost
        I guided you.
When you thought you were alone
        I brought you home.
I picked up the prayers
        you dropped on the rug.
 I became the talking stick
        you held in your hand.
Became the drum
        you could not stop beating.
Wherever you go I am there.
You carry me—a waxing moon
        at your back.

Total Solar Eclipse, 2024

Finally
I stood
watching
the ragged
moon
slip away

The sun
shone
full again
like
a resurrection

When
I removed
the dark glasses
I saw
a bumblebee
hovering close
to my face

How long
she had been there
beside me
silent
as the birds
I could
not say

Notes

"A Way into the Trees": Italicized line is from A. E. Housman's "Loveliest of trees, the cherry now."

"Cold Long Night": December's full moon was named the Cold Moon and Long Night Moon by Native Americans. See also Elizabeth Landau's article, "Symphony of stars: The science of stellar sound waves," July 30, 2018, https://science.nasa.gov/universe/exoplanets/symphony-of-stars-the-science-of-stellar-sound-waves.

"Collage for a Friend in Grief": While other writers have expressed this thought, in stanza one I am thinking of Louise Glück's "Nostos" and "An Adventure." Stanza two alludes to Anderson's play, *I Never Sang for my Father.* The third stanza blends lines from "Indelible" by Edward Hirsch.

"Each Morning, the Fall": Line seven echoes "The wind in the pines plays a stringless lute" by Dogen Zenji.

"I Asked Rilke's Darkest Angels": The words "guttering candle" and "deep unknown" are from Denise Levertov's "Mass for the Day of St. Thomas Didymus," the Kyrie section; "sheen of light" is from Rilke's "Leaving."

"It can happen anywhere": Reference Edward O. Wilson, "The Little Things That Run the World: The Importance and Conservation of Invertebrates," Address given at the opening of the invertebrate exhibit, National Zoological Park, Washington, D.C., on May 7, 1987.

"Reading Time": A haibun. In the haiku ending, I was inspired by Wang Wei's "A Green Stream." By addressing Basho, I aim to draw three cultures together.

"Remembering Linda Pastan": Italicized words in the last stanza are from Pastan's poem "October Funeral."

"Song for the Sea Lion, Steep Ravine CA" and "Remembering Miroslav Holub": The phrase *from some symphonic distance* is from Miroslav Holub's poem, "The Whale," in *Rampage.*

"To the Reader": The quotation by Margaret Gibson is from *Westerly Sun*, June 17, 2021, https://www.thewesterlysun.com/lifestyle/entertainment/the-arts-cafe-mystic-presents-a-green-poetry-cafe-with-margaret-gibson-and-friends/article_497a3130-9c88-11eb-a6b0-1fb6963641ae.html.

"We Came to a Place that Was Grieving and Gathered to Listen": The line "All this was a long time ago" is from "Journey of the Magi" by T. S. Eliot.

"When the Challenge Came in Fifth Grade": Italicized line attributed to Lao Tzu.

"Words": Italicized words are from Robert Hass, "Calm," in *Human Wishes*.

"You Entered My Car Years Later": The line "This moment is the best the world can give" is from Edna St. Vincent Millay's "Sonnet 69."

Poem Dedications

"A Way into the Trees": for Maureen Ryan Griffin

"Adobe House,Taos": in memory of my father, Raleigh Lee Blair

"Cicada, I Never Knew You Were the Loudest Insect in the World Until I Read": for Nancy Dorrier

"Collage for a Friend in Grief": for Ione O'Hara

"During the Time of No Moon:" for my niece Janet Blair

"The House within a Mansion": in memory of my parents and my brothers, Ralph, Ronnie and Ray

"Joy": for Eike and Helmut Diebold

"Maybe It Was Nott": for Patrick Crawford

"Milkweed, Jonas Ridge NC": for Susan

"Moon": for Gill Holland

"Octopus Farming for the Food Harvest": for Angelina Korinis

"Song for the Sea Lion": for my niece Monica Diebold

"Tea at My Potter Friend's *Wind Gather* Cabin, Jonas Ridge NC": for Maureen McGregor

"Ten Years Old and She No Longer Believes in Santa": for my great niece Brittney

"When You See a Shelf Mushroom": for Jim and Becky Keenan

"We Came to a Place that was Grieving and Gathered to Listen": in memory of my mother, Laura Pierce Blair

Acknowledgments

Heartfelt appreciation to:

Erica Fielder, artist, who graciously granted permission for me to use her watercolor *Mountains of the Moon* as the cover art for the book. I bought the painting in the 1980s on my first trip to Mendocino. In 2024 when I inquired about the inspiration for the painting, she replied: "I must have painted it in Alaska way up above the Arctic Circle on a kayak trip, or at least it was inspired by paintings from that trip." That place was called Mountains of the Moon. Find it, if you can!

Janet Blair, my niece, for insightful suggestions on many of these poems. Your loving support at this time remains immeasurable.

Patrick Crawford, friend and classmate, who walked the same streets as I did from elementary school throughout high school. When our paths met again, you offered encouragement and understood how "memories bump against each other, each deserving one last moment."

Richard Allen Taylor and Ann Campanella, outstanding writers and compassionate readers, for devoting so much of your time to providing perceptive, in-depth critiques of the manuscript.

Friends and poets who provided feedback over the years and who influenced revisions of some of these poems from their inception, including—though not limited to—Angelina Korinis, Martha Cox, Rebecca Schenck, Leslie Tompkins, Mary Anne Thomas, Maureen Ryan Griffin, Ione O'Hara, Diana Pinckney, Mary Kratt, Mary Crews, and the late Eleanor Brawley.

The dedicated team at Charlotte Lit Press. Many thanks to Paul Reali for his patience and technical expertise in the design and layout of this book. Enormous gratitude to Editor in Chief Kathie Collins, a woman of vision who, among her many gifts to the writing community, established the Press, believed in this book, and offered extensive critiques that sharpened its focus.

Deep gratitude to the editors of the following journals, anthologies and online publications in which these poems first appeared, sometimes in different form:

Black Moon Journal, Issue 6, April 2022
"Beyond the Iron Gate"
"Talking to Siri in Pandemic Time"

Book of Matches, Issue 11, May 2024
"Maybe It Was Nott"

Charlotte Viewpoint
"Poetry Reading at an Indian Trail Cafe," April 2011
"Email Morning," March 2012

Crossing the Rift: North Carolina Poets on 9/12 & Its Aftermath (2021, Press 53)
"Song for the Hours"

Drifting Sands: A Journal of Haibun and Tanka Prose, October 27, 2023
"Haibun — Reading Time"

Kakalak
"Salt," 2023
"One Peppermint Ball," 2021, Honorable Mention
"Cicada, I Never Knew You Were the Loudest Insect in the World Until I Read," 2021

Pinesong Awards — North Carolina Poetry Society, 2024
"Tea at My Potter Friend's *Wind Gather* Cabin, Jonas Ridge NC"
— Robert Golden Award, Honorable Mention

Sunspot Literary Journal, Vol 4, Issue 3, 2022
"We Came to a Place that was Grieving and Gathered to Listen"

Sunspot Geminga Contest, 2023
"Moon" — Finalist

Vine Leaves Literary Journal: A Collection of Vignettes from Across the Globe (2017, Vine Leaves Press)
"Words"

About the Author

Born in Jacksonville, FL, Irene Blair Honeycutt, award-winning poet and teacher, is the author of four previously published poetry books. Her debut collection won Sandstone Publishing's New South Poetry Book Regional Contest. Her third book, *Before the Light Changes* (Main Street Rag), was a finalist for the Brockman-Campbell Book Award.

During her long tenure at Central Piedmont Community College in Charlotte, NC, she received the Award for Excellence in Teaching and founded the Spring Literary Festival (later named Sensoria), which had a twenty-nine-year run. Other honors include the college's Irene Blair Honeycutt Distinguished Lectureship, and the Irene Blair Honeycutt Lifetime Achievement and Legacy Awards, established in her name.

In support of her writing, Honeycutt received a Creative Fellowship from the Charlotte Arts and Science Council. A North Carolina Arts Council Scholarship provided her an opportunity to study with Miroslav Holub at the Prague Summer Writers Workshop in the Czech Republic. She also has studied with David Whyte in Ireland and with Bill Holm in Iceland. She still fondly recalls lessons she learned at her first ever major writing conference at Bread Loaf under the tutelage of Mark Strand and Linda Pastan and from conversations between them that she overheard in the hallways. And she remembers with gratitude two regional poets whose workshops first encouraged her to publish: Bennie Lee Sinclair, South Carolina's fifth poet laureate; and Susan Ludvigson, poet and recipient of Guggenheim and Fulbright Fellowships.

Honeycutt's advocacy of writers has been acknowledged by the community at large. She received the Best of Charlotte Award from *Creative Loafing* for Best Contribution to the Improvement of Charlotte's Literary Climate. For her service to the Charlotte Writers Club, she received the Adelia Kimball Founder's Award. In 2023, *Storied Charlotte* included her among "Six Women Who've Shaped the History of Charlotte's Community of Readers and Writers."

A teacher at heart, Honeycutt teaches in various venues, including Charlotte Lit, and mentors individual writers. She believes that poetry, while it cannot save us, contributes a positive force to society and to our lives, fostering hope and healing.

Printed in the USA
CPSIA information can be obtained
at www.ICGtesting.com
LVHW040434081224
798391LV00002B/52